THE KING PENGUIN BOOKS

59

ACKERMANN'S CAMBRIDGE

£2

A memento of
Cambridge.

17 : vi : 52.

ACKERMANN'S

CAMBRIDGE

BY

Reginald Ross Williamson

———

WITH TWENTY
COLOURED PLATES FROM
*A History of the
University of Cambridge,
its Colleges, Halls and
Public Buildings*

1815

Penguin Books

———

LONDON

THE KING PENGUIN BOOKS

Editor : N. B. L. Pevsner
Technical Editor : R. B. Fishenden

First published 1951

Text printed by
R. & R. Clark Ltd, Edinburgh
Plates made and printed by
John Swain & Son Ltd, Barnet
Cover design by William Grimmond
Made in Great Britain

ACKERMANN'S CAMBRIDGE

A History of the University of Cambridge, its Colleges, Halls and Public Buildings, was published in two volumes in 1815 by Rudolph Ackermann. Mr John Summerson has paid tribute to this remarkable man in his admirable introduction to *The Microcosm of London* published in this series. Born in Saxony in 1764, Ackermann spent ten years of his life practising as a saddler and coachbuilder in various German cities, in Paris and in London, before he set up a print shop in the Strand in 1795. Here he established a lithographic press which was to issue, year after year, an astonishing series of illustrated works. They range from the comprehensive *The Repository of Arts, Literature, Fashions*, etc., in forty volumes and *The World in Miniature* in forty-three volumes to the specialized topographical treatises of which this is one.

In the previous year Ackermann had brought out his history of the University of Oxford. This had been so great a success that he, always an astute business man, had immediately embarked upon the obvious sequel. He was not disappointed. He could engage the same team of illustrators, that superb trio among them: Pugin, Mackenzie and Westall, whose united efforts raised, under his patronage, British lithographic art to its finest manifestation. Augustus Charles Pugin, whose most important work of this kind appears in *The Microcosm of London*, was, possibly, the best of all Ackermann's illustrators. A French *émigré* who escaped from a country made unendurable, in his opinion, by the

Revolution, he was to have almost as great an influence on nineteenth-century English architecture as his more famous son, A. W. N. Pugin, chiefly remembered today as the co-designer with Barry of the Palace of Westminster. Soon after he arrived here from France he became a draughtsman in the office of the fashionable architect John Nash. He was set to work making coloured perspective views of those mansions in the Gothic style which his master had in hand at the time. They were so good that Nash commissioned him to produce a series of drawings of genuinely ancient buildings which might form a corpus of material for future designs. It is the veracity of these drawings which attracted so much attention and which, of course, made him such an admirable topographical artist. His study of authentic detail was to have a great effect on those phases of the Gothic Revival which succeeded the 'Strawberry Hill' period; the change-over from the 'Romantic' to the 'Academic' appreciation of mediaeval architecture is due very largely to the careful drawings of the Elder Pugin. Frederick Mackenzie, who 'covered' the Coronation of King George IV, but was much more interested in purely architectural subjects, published his *Observations on the Construction of the Roof of King's College Chapel, Cambridge,* in 1846 – more than thirty years after he had contributed six plates on this same college to our volumes. Towards the end of his life he was to suffer as one of the first of the British nineteenth-century book illustrators to be affected by the new medium of photography. William Westall, friend of Southey and Wordsworth, was appointed at the age of eighteen by the President of the Royal Academy, Benjamin West, to be official landscape draughtsman to an expedition to Australia under the command of Matthew Flinders. He was shipwrecked, suffered the appropriate privations, but produced, as a result of his wanderings, drawings which are among the finest

6

products of English lithographic art. His early experience did not deter him from further journeys to distant countries, and his observations were recorded in beautiful books about China, India, New South Wales, Jamaica and Madeira.

The plates of Ackermann's Cambridge as they stand, at least the sixty-four topographical ones, of which, alas, only less than a third could here be reproduced, would make a fairly practical guide to the University of today, for the major landmarks of Cambridge have not been altered between Ackermann's time and our own. It is true that those manifestations of the Gothic Revival which form a salient feature of the Cambridge scene today do not appear in any of our plates. Rickman's New Court across the river at St John's, and the Bridge of Sighs with which his partner Hutchinson connected it to the ancient courts (perhaps the most famous view in Cambridge after the King's Chapel-Clare College ensemble) were not to begin until 1826. Wilkins's New Court at Corpus, his Screen and Entrance Gate at King's, Blore's Pitt Press, Wyatt's remodelling of Sidney and, later on still, Scott's great Chapel at St John's, are all things of the future. The Cambridge we see in these plates is practically untouched by the impending Revival of the Gothic; the decoration of both halls and chapels appears predominantly Classical. Still, those differences between our plates and the Cambridge with which we are familiar are comparatively small. The building and planning traditions which Ackermann records are still those of today.

Another tradition also happily survives. It goes back much further than the nineteenth century and may perhaps be said to connect the Cambridge of our day more closely with the Middle Ages than with 1815: the tradition of learning and civilized living. The Cambridge we see in our plates was the Cambridge of privilege. The Royal Commissions of enquiry

7

and their resultant reforms were still far ahead in the future. Scholarship, indolence and eccentricity were commonly encouraged under the prevailing system of patronage and endowment; individual character made the choice and each commanded respect. It was possible to obtain at this time – and for many years afterwards – a life fellowship of a college at the age of twenty-one and to live for ever afterwards in superb comfort, to dine daily at as good a table as there was in England, to enjoy the respect of the young – and, if you desired, to become thoroughly nasty. As an example of privilege – and one cited only because its observance became an almost classic grievance – was the procedure which allowed members of King's College to become Bachelors of Arts without presenting themselves for examination. Mathematics was the only subject in which it was possible to take a 'Tripos', or Honours, Degree. The Classical Tripos was not to be established until 1824, although, of course, a knowledge of ancient languages was commonly assumed. Those proceeding to it were mostly destined for the Established Church, the Law and Medicine. A respectable number, however, returned to administer their own lands. Roman Catholics and Nonconformists were excluded from the University altogether. There were under a thousand members in residence – a fifth of the number today. The mediaeval tradition of monasticism was observed by the imposition of celibacy as a qualification for fellowship of a college. Otherwise the occupations which were to be frowned upon before the century was out – drinking, gambling, street-fighting and downright laziness – were among the more obvious dissipations of the generation which inhabited the Cambridge of our plates. Yet the serious pursuit of learning, which had been the reason of the University's existence for six centuries, was quietly persistent. This is so today. In a world where the word 'Cambridge' is synonymous with the development of poison gases, bacterial warfare and atomic energy there is abundant evidence that an interest in the Humanities still flourishes.

This is the oldest of the Cambridge Colleges. Its foundation in 1284, by Hugh de Balsham, Bishop of Ely, took place only a few years after that of Merton, Oxford's senior college. Hence it is 'Oxford and Cambridge' rather than the other way about. But it is not because of its age that Peterhouse, as it is now called (but never, in any circumstances, 'Peterhouse College'), is important in the history of the University; it was the first time that a break was made from the established idea that the benefits of a college education might be enjoyed only by those intending to take monastic orders. Probably most of the inmates of the new college did become monks eventually, or at least took Orders, but it is not laid down in the statutes that this was essential. It is difficult for us today to realize what an advance in emancipation this was. Peterhouse is the first college the traveller will see as he comes into Cambridge along the road from London. Architecturally, he will almost certainly be disappointed; the splendid Fitzwilliam Museum, which he has passed a hundred yards or so before, invites an anti-climax. It is a pity that twenty-two years had yet to go before Basevi had anything to show of this great classical revival Portland-stone masterpiece which houses one of the best provincial collections in Britain. Behind its grandeur lies the miniature Deer Park of Peterhouse, lovely and unexpected. The architecturally curious will, however, soon discover that the college, for all its demureness, possesses that

9

rarity: a specimen of the Gothic survival. It was built in 1630. The first ecstasies of the Renaissance were long over and it is rather as though a compromise had been wrought with it by the obsolete but respectable Gothic, itself practically dead a hundred years or more. The result is uneasy – absurd, if you like – but it is one of the things the art-historian will cherish most in Cambridge. The east window, seen in our picture, is filled by the original glass which carries out a design by Rubens. The building was commissioned by Dr Matthew Wren who, many years later, we shall meet as the instigator of Pembroke College Chapel across the road. By his 'going behind the Reformation' in designing this chapel, he incurred Puritan wrath; it was unforgivable to crowd 'so much Popery in so small a chapel'.

The red-brick gable this side of the Chapel belongs to the Library. The date inscribed in the cartouche is 1633, the year in which the wing was extended to the street front although the chamber proper was finished some forty years before. On the other side is the Fellows' Building, designed by Sir James Burrough and built between 1738 and 1742. Burrough was Master of Caius between 1754 and 1764. He is one of the most distinguished of the Cambridge architects. We shall meet his work often in our perambulation. One of the first people to live in this building was Thomas Gray, who had rooms in the top storey. We shall look out of his window in Plate 3.

Do not let us overlook the sheep, the cow, wending southward out of Cambridge market. The town, as much today as when these views were made, is the centre of one of the richest agricultural areas in England. Cambridge Market is still an important function in East Anglia today. The runlets of water along either side of the street are among the benefactions conferred upon the town by Thomas Hobson, Mayor of Cambridge in the seventeenth century. This was the famous monopolist of the carrier service between the town and London – hence 'Hobson's Choice'. The water, of an excellent quality, comes from the 'Nine Wells', some springs in the chalk belt, three miles to the southward, and eventually gushes out of the fountain in the Market Place.

PLATE 2 : CLARE HALL

This is the most famous of all Cambridge prospects. It is, in fact, *Cambridge* for all the multitudes who have never been there, knowing it only from that endless series of 'views' of which, presumably, this is the prototype. The quality of design, the excellence of masonry, the great lawn, the weeping willows, Thomas Rumbold's slightly wilting bridge are the chief components in the design. Only King's Chapel, just 'out of picture' to the right, is missing. All the same, Pugin has avoided that sentimental approach to his subject to which so many of his successors succumbed. The languorous river of today is shown here doing the job of work which it performed for many centuries: chief constituent in the Port of Cambridge. Those wherries have, most likely, come up the Cam from Ely, or they may have come from as far off as King's Lynn by way of the Great Ouse. They are, in any case, almost within sight of their destination. The wide pools, dominated since 'Domesday Book' by the King's and Bishop's Mills, are a few hundred yards upstream. There terminates the navigable water; Grantchester Mill, of equal fame since Chaucer's day, is another three miles upstream – but weirs intrude. Punt and canoe bring profitable return to the Cambridge ship-owner of today but, so late as our artists' visit, a legitimate mercantile trade was still being pursued.

Clare College was founded in 1338 by Lady Clare, grand-

11

daughter of Edward I and sister-in-law of Piers Gaveston. We can see in our picture more easily than we can in life the western façade as it was built. The trees which obscure it so much today had not yet grown up. The homogeneity of design in the building is unequalled in Cambridge. The architect – or 'builder', as he was not ashamed to describe himself – was Robert Grumbold, nephew of the Grumbold who built the bridge and received 3s. for the design of it. The work was done between 1669 and 1705. The stone came from the famous oolitic limestone quarries of Weldon and Ketton in Rutland. The slates are from the equally renowned and neighbouring Colley Weston. The great lawn, of which we see only a corner, belongs to King's College. To appreciate the quality of one of the classic lawns of Britain the visitor should climb to the roof of King's Chapel and look down upon it from there.

PLATE 3 : PEMBROKE HALL

We have moved up Trumpington Street, on the road from London, about 100 yards from the spot where Pugin drew Plate 1, and his collaborator, Mackenzie, has climbed to that window (or a very near neighbour) on the northern side of the Fellows' Building in Peterhouse where the poet Thomas Gray lived. Gray was terrified of fire and arranged a life-saving apparatus which he attached to the iron bar normally supporting the window-box in which he grew mignonette. Undergraduates shouting 'Fire! Fire!' and their mockery when he descended his ropes into a tub of water caused him to move across the street to Pembroke. We look down into the graveyard of St Mary the Less or 'Little St Mary's' as it is generally called. Perhaps it is a pity that the artist did not extend his angle of vision to the left to show us the lovely east window of the church itself whose containing gable encloses the view.

The church, completed in 1352, is the best thing of its kind in Cambridge. It may have been built by Alan of Walsingham, sacrist of Ely, who was responsible for the Lady Chapel in the Cathedral there and organized the building of its timber octagonal lantern, one of the marvels of our Perpendicular style of architecture. American visitors usually make this little church a point of pilgrimage because of its association with the family of Washington; a monument to Richard Washington, incumbent in the early eighteenth century, bears the arms of the family. Our illustrator, however, has done his duty instead by the chapel of Pembroke College on the far side of the street. This is, except for a doorway in Ely Cathedral, the earliest work by Christopher Wren. It dates from 1663, and its beginning marked the ending of eighteen years' imprisonment in the Tower of London under the Puritan regime of Wren's uncle, the Bishop of Ely. Dr Matthew Wren had been a Fellow of Pembroke years before and then had become Master of Peterhouse and responsible for the Jacobean Gothic chapel we have seen in Plate 1. On his release from captivity he set about the building of this very different work for his original college. Pembroke was founded in 1347 by Marie de Valence, Countess of Pembroke. Among its most famous members were Edmund Spenser and the younger Pitt. Bisected in our picture by the farther gable of the college is the tower of St Botolph's Church. St Botolph was an East Anglian abbot of the Benedictine Order and a favourite patron of travellers; hence the number of churches dedicated to him at the gates of mediaeval cities.[1] This particular church adjoined the southern entrance to Cambridge. To the east-

1. London has four: in Aldgate, Aldersgate, Bishopsgate and Billingsgate.

ward is the tower of St Benet, whose Saxon masonry is the oldest work in the town and, to the eastward again, the late Perpendicular tower, begun in 1593, of St Mary the Great, the University Church. From this tower issue, every quarter-hour, the original Cambridge Chimes. They were composed by Dr Jowett of Trinity Hall about 1790 and are said to be an adaptation of Handel's 'I know that my Redeemer liveth'. Curfew is tolled every evening on the Great Bell of the peal, formerly of practical value in the safe guiding of beleaguered travellers in the neighbouring fenland. It is also used to summon 'Congregations' (sessions of the legislative body of the University) in the Senate House opposite. But the climax of this picture, as it is of so many Cambridge vistas, is the tremendous bulk of King's College Chapel. This distant view does not exist today ; the French Gothic tower of the Congregational Church takes the place of the seven-teenth-century timber-framed houses and beyond it rises the tower of the Pitt Press – the Cambridge University Press. Seventeen years after our picture was done, Edward Blore (best known, perhaps, by his work at Lambeth Palace) built his mock-Gothic factory – a rather idealized conception of what a Cambridge college ought to look like. The money to pay for it was left over from a subscription raised to erect a statue to the Younger Pitt in Hanover Square – hence its title.

PLATE 4 : CAIUS COLLEGE

Gonville and Caius College is the proper title today. In 1348, a year after Pembroke was founded, Edmund Gonville of Norfolk endowed a theological institute in Free School Lane which was named after him. To this, in 1529, was admitted a student called Caius who later became Fellow of the college.

14

Later still he became physician in turn to Edward VI, Mary Tudor and Elizabeth. Today he is remembered as one of the great 'characters' in English medicine. In 1557 he re-founded his old college and its name thereafter became coupled with his own. Today Caius is first and foremost a medical college – as its re-founder intended it to be. Architecturally, it is chiefly famous for its three symbolic gateways, of Humility, Virtue and Honour. Through the last of these, an exquisite piece of early English Renaissance work, the suppliant for a degree passes from his college to its conferment in the Senate House which we see beyond.

PLATE 5 : TRINITY HALL

It has always been difficult to get a fair view of this famous law college. The modern photographer has been no more successful than his predecessor, the print-maker. Its front entrance opens upon an ancient lane whose narrowness defeats even the wide-angle lens. This is a pity because insufficient justice has been awarded to its designer, Sir James Burrough, whose work we have already seen at Peterhouse (Plate 1). In this, his own college, he built the Front Court. The stone came from Ketton. The arms in the pediment are those of the college, which was founded in 1350 by William Bateman, Bishop of Norwich. The complex of ancient buildings which fills the left-hand side of the plate is the Old Court of King's College. This was, for nearly three centuries, the sole secular part of the college, whose superb chapel appears in the background. The contrast between these buildings of a 'poor and unsubstantial character' (Willis and Clarke) and the chief glory of the University, is very marked. Nevertheless, this was 'King's' from 1447 until

Gibbs built his range in 1723. The site was bought by the University authorities in 1829 in order to extend the Library. Among the architects invited to compete for the new building were Decimus Burton, Cockerell, Rickman and Wilkins. Cockerell won but, owing to lack of funds with which to carry out his ambitious designs, only the north side was built. In 1840 the parapets of King's Chapel were finally obscured from this particular viewpoint, but the two western pinnacles still soar above Cockerell's building. Still to be seen, as it is in our plate, is the south-east corner of Clare College Chapel. Again by the hand of Burrough, it was built in 1765.

PLATE 6: KING'S COLLEGE CHAPEL

This is the supreme architectural ornament of Cambridge, and one of the great buildings of England. With St George's, Windsor, the Chapel at Eton – the sister foundation of King's – and Henry VII's Chapel at Westminster it forms a group in which the final expression of the Perpendicular period of Gothic architecture was achieved. The majesty of the fan-vaulted roof, the huge area of window space filled, for the greater part, with its original glass, the quality of the wood-work of Renaissance organ and choir stalls are too well known to need comment here. Yet some critics have suggested that the mass-produced decoration of Tudor Roses, Antelope Supporters and Portcullises, and the mathematically correct construction weary the discerning eye with repetition and perfection. It is only its scale that saves it, they say; size has intimidated the timid critic. The chapel is the only part which came to anything out of all the grandiose schemes for his royal foundation devised by King Henry VI. There were to have been great courts and a campanile in scale with the chapel.

But the wretched court we saw in Plate 4 was as far as accommodation went until the eighteenth century. The chapel was probably begun in 1448. The king, we know, was responsible for most of the designs, but it is likely that Reginald of Ely was the actual interpreter. The stone came from the college's own quarry in Thefdale, Thoresdale, south-west of Tadcaster in Yorkshire, and from the neighbouring Hudleston, about a mile west of Sherburn. Both these quarries are in the Lower Magnesian Limestone. The stone was brought to Cambridge by the rivers Wharfe, Yorkshire Ouse and Humber, then across the Wash to King's Lynn and so on up the Great Ouse and Cam. These sources of supply seem to have become exhausted in 1455, whereupon things were more or less at a standstill until 1476. Then a fresh effort was made to complete the five eastern bays of the choir – those we see in the foreground of our plate. The stone in this case was brought from Peterborough, from Clipsham in Rutland, and from Weldon in Northamptonshire and the timber from Ashdon, Thaxted and Canfield in Essex. The seven bays to the west, whose walls at this time were only about ten feet high, remained unfinished until 1506. The enormous vault was begun in 1512 and the whole fabric finished three years later. The master mason of this later period was John Wastell. It was he who designed the Bell Harry Tower of Canterbury Cathedral.

Then began the business of glazing the twenty-six windows – perhaps the biggest single job of its kind hitherto attempted. Bernard Flower, the Royal glazier, worked on the scheme for ten years, and he was succeeded by Galyon Hoone of Southwark, Richard Bownde of St. Clement Danes, Reeve of St Sepulchre and Symonds of St Margaret's, Westminster. The only window not included in the series is the west one; that was finished some three hundred years later, of bits and pieces.

17

We are looking towards the east window. Its subject is the Crucifixion.

The organ screen, darker today than it appears in our picture, which divides the chapel from the ante-chapel, was constructed in 1533–35. Like everything else in the building it is of huge size. It is carved, pretty well all over, with Renaissance motifs and the royal cyphers of A.R. (Anna Regina) and H.A. (Henricus, Anna) show that it was built while Anne Boleyn was queen. The organ itself was finished by Renatus Harris in 1688 and enlarged by John Avery in 1803.[1]

To appreciate to the full the structure of this great building the enquirer should climb the staircase in one of the four corner turrets to the false, or inner, roof and there inspect the obverse aspect of the fan-vaulting, the gigantic chestnut carpentry of this impressive, unswept, draughty, pigeon-haunted scene. Afterwards, he should go up to the sunshine of the leaden roof proper. Our Plate is by Pugin, but Mackenzie, a fellow member of Ackermann's team of illustrators, made a special study of the roof which he published in 1846.[2]

PLATE 7 : CATHERINE HALL CHAPEL

St Catherine's College was founded in 1473 by Robert Woodlark, Provost of King's. But the college as we see it here and as we see it today dates from two centuries later. Like Clare, the homogeneity of the buildings is almost complete; there is no hugger-mugger mediaeval complex here for the

1. The Choir of King's College, Cambridge, is among the most renowned of its kind.
2. *Observations on the Construction of the Roof of King's College Chapel, Cambridge.*

18

antiquarian to sentimentalize over. The central block was begun in 1674 by Richard Grumbold – we have met the family before at Clare – and was finished in 1757 by James Essex to virtually the original design. The chapel, whose interior we see here, is part of the general plan. It was consecrated in 1704 by the Bishop of Ely. We know very little about its furnishings; John Austin was paid £353 for making the woodwork and Thomas Woodward a further £30 for carving certain parts of it. All of it is satisfactory enough. Protestants will approve the dressings of the altar. The date of our drawing, they should remember, is 1815.

PLATE 8 : BENET COLLEGE CHAPEL

The visitor will look in vain for Benet College. He had better ask for 'Corpus'. Then he may arrive at Corpus Christi College, founded in 1352 by the Guilds of Corpus Christi and of the Blessed Virgin for the education of priests to sing masses for past members. From its foundation the members of the college had used the ancient church, with its Saxon tower (see Plate 3), dedicated to St Benedict (hence the abbreviated St Benet), as its chapel, until, in 1579, Sir Nicholas Bacon, Lord Keeper of the Great Seal of England, agreed with the Society to build a new one. In the picture we see the chapel as it was in 1815 ; the old building had been 'fitted up with great neatness and elegance' in 1742 under the surveillance of Burrough (see Plates 1 and 4). The most noticeable thing about it is the flat ceiling with its plaster pendants which were reputed to be identical with those at Trinity College. We see three coats of arms carved in the wainscoting; they are, from left to right, those of Manners, Duke of Rutland, the College, and a Master called Jegon. But all this disappeared, and a great deal else besides, to make room for the new chapel and the New Court which were begun in 1823. Wilkins was the designer, an architect of whose work we see as much today as we do of Burrough's although, at the time our plates were engraved, he had not much to point to in Cambridge.[1] Perhaps his most successful piece in the University is the eastern screen to the court of King's College – on the opposite side of the street. Visitors who do not enjoy neo-Gothic architecture must console themselves with an all the more thorough inspection of Archbishop Parker's Library, one of the most famous college libraries anywhere. Among its most obvious treasures are the Gospel Book used by St Augustine in his missionary campaign among the English and Alfred the Great's own copy of the Anglo-Saxon Chronicle. The library was saved from the rubbish heap by the first Protestant Primate of Canterbury, who afterwards became Master of the college. The Old Court, dating from 1350 to 1360, is the oldest complete court in Cambridge.

PLATE 9: QUEENS' COLLEGE
(FROM THE PRIVATE WALK)

Queens' was established in 1448 by Margaret of Anjou, wife of Henry VI, founder of the neighbouring royal college. She was fifteen years old at the time; her husband was twenty-two when he made his own pious resolution to found the college now known as "King's". The re-establishment of the house by Elizabeth Woodville, wife of Edward IV, determines the position of the apostrophe in the title; two queens, as opposed to one at Oxford, beneficed this particu-

1. In London we have his National Gallery in Trafalgar Square and his University College in Gower Street.

lar royal foundation. The wherries in the foreground are engaged in the still extensive mercantile river traffic of the town. They are little different in design from their successors in the Fenlands or Broads of East Anglia today. Some of the lime-trees originally planted in 1732 which so neatly border the formal walks still exist today, but the greater part have fallen in one famous gale or other – the most exacting gale in our time was that of 1916 – and as the result of disease.

We must also mention the turret on the right in which Erasmus lived from 1510 to 1513. He was one of the most influential people ever to have been in Cambridge. His arrival here, under the patronage of Fisher, later to become Bishop of Rochester, as the first teacher of Greek meant that the Middle Ages were over and the New Learning of the Renaissance had arrived. Erasmus was given the best rooms in the house, but hated them, the college and Cambridge. He grumbled without ceasing and was nostalgic for his native Rotterdam. The classical white brick façade which rises sheer from the river between the fence and the bridge and which was to have been extended along the entire riverside frontage of the college had there been money enough, was designed by Essex and built between 1756 and 1760.

PLATE 10 : CHRIST COLLEGE

The foundress of this college, in 1506, was Lady Margaret Beaufort, Countess of Richmond and of Derby, mother of King Henry VII. The great Fisher, whom we have met at Queens' (Plate 9), was her confessor and persuaded her to perform this pious act. Her name is honoured in perpetuity

21

in Cambridge by her endowment of the Lady Margaret Chair of Divinity. We shall meet her again at St John's College. The Entrance Gate, which we see here, bears her arms with their antelope supporters: Plantagenet roses, Beaufort portcullises and her own little marguerites. It has been suggested that this panel was designed by William Swayn and carved by Ralph Bolmore. The chamber above the gate has always been the Muniment Room – or Treasury – of the college. What we see here is part of the early buildings which, together with most of the first Court, were built within a few years of the foundation. Alas, it was constructed of the local hard chalk – or clunch – which does not last; in 1714 the front of the college was the first part to undergo a re-casing in 'freestone', which is, in most cases, stone from Ketton. The visitor should not miss the Fellows' Building, one of the most distinguished pieces of Cambridge architecture. Nobody seems to know who was its designer – popularly it is ascribed to Inigo Jones – but it is accepted that it was built between 1640 and 1642. Possibly one of the Rumbold family, whose activities we have already seen at Clare (Plate 2) and at St Catherine's (Plate 7), may have had a hand in it; certainly its style is reminiscent of the family's previous work. It is unlikely that the visitor will avoid being shown the famous mulberry tree associated with John Milton, a member of the college, in the Fellows' Garden, but he should not miss the Cold Bath, surrounded by its miniature wilderness and overlooked by portrait busts on pedestals – one of them is Milton's. Nor should he overlook the beautiful and rare dual monument to Sir Thomas Finch and Sir Thomas Baines in the chapel, the work of Joseph Catterns. The runlets of water we see in our view are branch streams of Hobson's Conduit, whose main stream we saw flowing along Trumpington Street in Plate 1. They feed the Cold Bath and the swimming pool at the neighbouring Emmanuel College. Charles Darwin, one of the most famous sons of this house, came into residence here fourteen years after Ackermann's volumes had been published – in the same year as Tennyson and Thackeray 'came up'.

PLATE 11: TRINITY COLLEGE KITCHEN

The history of the construction of the Kitchen and the great Hall of the college which it serves has been preserved in a separate Account Book now kept among the precious manuscripts in the Library. From it we learn that the architect was Ralph Symons – who we shall meet again at St John's College – and that the foundations were laid on Thursday July 7th, 1605. Most of the stone came from the local clunch quarries at Barrington, the limestone – for dressings – from King's Cliffe in Northamptonshire; a certain amount of old material from Cambridge Castle was used for the core of the walls. So much for these facts about the building. As to what went on inside, it would be fascinating to compute the immense amount of superb food which had been prepared in this splendid room before our drawing was made, establishing a tradition which was to be continually and increasingly honoured for at least another century and a quarter.

PLATE 12: TRINITY COLLEGE GREAT COURT

Trinity is the largest college in either university. It was founded in 1546 by King Henry VIII as a rival to Cardinal Wolsey's foundation of Christ Church at Oxford. Its Master

is appointed by the Crown, and among the holders of distinguished benefactions are the Regius Professors of Divinity,
Hebrew and Greek. We are in the Great Court[1] and get a
good idea of its immense size – over 90,000 square feet. To
encircle it while the clock on the left strikes twelve is one of
the stock feats of undergraduate prowess. It is true that the
hour is struck twice, first on the biggest of the three tower
bells, whose note is A flat, and secondly on E flat. This
arrangement is supposed to be solely one of convenience :
it has been successfully contended that the absorbed
listener may miss the first stroke or two proclaiming the
hour. The distance to be run is 383 yards and the time
taken by the double chimes is 43 seconds – and there are
four corners to negotiate. The clock is in the 'Edward III
Gateway', finished in 1437 and carefully moved back
in 1600 from its original site when the present dimensions
of the Court were projected. The shields of arms to the
left and right of the arch are those of England and of Henry
VI. The statue above, an Elizabethan copy of the original
one, is of Edward III. The arms of the college are below it.
On either side of the clock face are the arms of France and
England. The bell turret was reconstructed in 1856–57. The
room below the clock face houses the college muniments.
Adjoining the tower is the chapel, built by Queen Mary soon
after her accession.

Once past that – as it appears in our picture – steadfastly
closed and Protestant door the visitor will discover, a little to
his left hand, one of the few really first-class pieces of monu-
mental sculpture in Cambridge: Roubiliac's statue of Sir
Isaac Newton. Chantrey called it the noblest of English

1. Ackermann calls it Quadrangle, but quadrangle is an Oxford
term not used at Cambridge. Ackermann had finished his Oxford
volumes before he embarked on Cambridge.

24

statues; Wordsworth immortalized it in his description of the moonlit face, in the locked, silent chapel:

The marble index of a mind for ever
Voyaging through strange seas of thought alone.

The majestic Great Gate, on the right of our picture, is the grandest of all its kind in Cambridge. It was begun in 1518. The outer face is splendid in its heraldic carving but the side we see is simpler. King James I looks down from the central niche; on his right is his queen, Anne of Denmark; on his left, Prince Charles, his son. These figures were put up in 1615. The fountain, the central feature and chief glory of the Great Court, was begun in 1601–2. Nobody seems to know who designed it; we merely know that its foundation is of brick and the stone of the superstructure was quarried at King's Cliffe and Clipsham. Its supply of water has been continuous since 1325. Its source is a spring about three miles west of Cambridge on the road to Madingley. This court has seen many illustrious ceremonies; one of them, which took place about the time this plate was drawn, was the triumphal and hilarious procession of Field-Marshal Blücher in his carriage, drawn by admirers, round the entire circuit on the occasion of his receiving an honorary degree. That was in the year before Waterloo.

PLATE 13 : TRINITY COLLEGE LIBRARY

The design of this vast and splendid library was given free by Sir Christopher Wren. Its inspiration may have been the library of St Mark's at Venice, by Sansovino, which was built in 1536. Work here was begun in 1675 under Robert Grumbold, of the famous Cambridge family of masons and architects. He was paid four guineas a month for his labours. The stone, in many shades from pink to orange, came from the Oolitic Limestone belt of Ketton.

The cases were made by Cornelius Austin and the carving upon them was done by Grinling Gibbons in lime-wood between 1691 and 1693. The plaster-work of the ceiling and the walls was done by plasterers from London working under the direction of a Mr Banckes. The busts which surround the presses form a varied collection; the two we see on entering are those of Ray, the seventeenth-century naturalist, and his pupil Willoughby, both of them done by Roubiliac. But the most striking piece of statuary in the library today is the standing effigy of Byron at the far end of the aisle. It is by Thorwaldsen the Dane, and was intended for Westminster Abbey, but the Dean and Chapter refused it admittance there. Thirty years have yet to go before it makes an appearance in our scene. The painted window above the south end of the library is by William Peckitt of York. Our reduced scale is too small for us to appreciate it, alas. The design, which is by Cipriani, shows Sir Isaac Newton in the act of being presented to King George III by his Alma Mater. Peckitt was paid a hundred guineas for this design in 1775. Wren was particular about the furnishings of the library, and the table, desk and two stools allotted to each of the 'celles', as he calls them, which we see on either side, were executed to his designs. Although not visible in this drawing, it seems a pity, when such a team of great craftsmen are involved, not to mention the four statues on the eastern parapet of the library roof. They are by Gabriel Cibber and represent Divinity, Law, Physic and Mathematics. Cibber himself, who received £20 apiece for them, came down from London with his men to place them in position according to his liking.

PLATE 14 : JESUS COLLEGE FROM THE CLOSE

The College of Jesus, the Blessed Virgin Mary, St John the
Evangelist and St Radegund was founded in 1497 by John
Alcock, Bishop of Ely, on the site of a convent of Benedictines
which had been there since the eleventh century. Many other
Cambridge societies have either incorporated or succeeded
monastic foundations – events we have usually not had space
enough to record – but in this case it is particularly interesting to remember the origin of the house because of its
exceptionally fine chapel. We see its tower in the background
of our view; it was part of the original convent buildings and is
one of the most interesting pieces of early mediaeval architecture remaining in Cambridge today. The quality and scale of
its thirteenth-century workmanship are up to cathedral stand-
ard. A roof by Pugin, windows by Burne-Jones and Madox
Brown and a painted ceiling by William Morris are among the
benefactions it has received since Westall made this drawing
in 1814. The original Cloister, peculiar to the monastic plan,
remains unique in Cambridge. In our illustration we look
across to the Gate of Entrance, built by the Founder. Its
original effect is spoiled – for the purists – by the heightening
of the buildings on either side by the addition of a further
storey in 1718. The range on this side of the court was begun
in 1638 by the Master, Dr Richard Sterne. The range on the
far side of the Gate is part of the Master's Lodge. We face the
Library. Its bookcases were furnished by Edmund Boldero,
Master in the later part of the seventeenth century. The Close,
or Grove, from which this prospect is viewed, was first
planted with ash trees in 1590–91. The trees shown here are
obviously not of those; they are probably some of the 400
young plants which were put in between 1780 and 1782, when
the Grove was a more popular promenade than it is today.

Notice should be taken of the fowl which decorate the banks of the small watercourse in our picture. They are an indication of the enormous bird population of the Fens which still come up to and, indeed, encircle the town. Wild fowling was a sport widely indulged in Cambridge long after Ackermann's time.

PLATE 15: ST JOHN'S COLLEGE SECOND COURT

Here again the pious Lady Margaret Beaufort and that great figure of the Renaissance, John Fisher, worked together to establish this college. In 1511, five years after she had founded Christ's College, the decayed Hospital of St John, then 300 years old and on its last legs, was replaced by her new foundation. She died before her plans were realized and it was due to Fisher's enormous exertions that the new college survived at all. Today it is second only to Trinity in its fame, population and architecture. Our plate shows only a part of this material wealth, but in its red-brick perfection the Second Court is unique in several ways. In the first case it is practically unaltered since it was built by Ralph Symons in 1598–1602. All the details relating to its construction, even plans and coloured elevations, survive and they are particularly extensive. Gilbert Wigg, of Cambridge, was Symons's partner in the enterprise. It was stipulated that the brick was to come from Stow in Norfolk – 'or in some other place where very good bricke is to be had'; the masonry where, from its position, it was particularly vulnerable to the weather was to be of 'Cliff free ston', *i.e.* from King's Cliffe in Northamptonshire, and the internal work was to be of a good 'whit ston, commonly called Barrington ston', *i.e.* clunch or the hard chalk which is quarried in the Cambridgeshire parish of that name.

The court was to cost £3400. It is important for the architectural historian to know that the agreement also stipulates that the new structure should resemble as much as possible the 'owlde buildinge' it replaced. An artificial time-lag must be imposed, therefore, in judging the date from its appearance.

The cost of this court was borne by Mary Cavendish, Countess of Shrewsbury, whose statue of 1671, by Thomas Burman, looks down from its niche over the gateway. Do not let us overlook the group of humble bed-makers, or 'bedders', beside the gateway turret. It is their duty to make the beds and otherwise tend the chambers of undergraduates. They are, by a University Statute which seeks to diminish temptation, selected from the ranks of those who are 'senex et horrida ex aetate'. So many great men have been members of this college, which for centuries rivalled Trinity in point of size and fame, that an attempt to make even a short list of them would be invidious. But Wordsworth, if only because of his description of the college in 'The Prelude', must be mentioned.

PLATE 16 : MAGDALENE COLLEGE LIBRARY

Magdalene – the final 'e' distinguishes it from the Oxford college of similar dedication – was founded by Thomas, Lord Audley, in 1542. His descendant is always the College Visitor, having the right to appoint the Master, and the great house of the family at Audley End is a familiar sight to travellers on the old Cambridge Road which goes to London by way of Saffron Walden. The inscription above the central arch of the arcade says 'Bibliotheca Pepysiana 1724' and above that is carved the arms of Samuel Pepys and his motto 'Mens cujusque is est quisque' ('Each man's mind is his very self'). Here, in an

29

upper room, is Pepys's own collection of books which he formed in his London house in the presses he designed for them. In certain cases, when a volume was not tall enough to bring its top in alignment with its neighbours, Pepys had little bases made upon which they might stand to obtain this required extra height. Everything in the library remains as its founder intended; his own Diary is among the many treasures preserved here. The building was obviously built long before the date inscribed upon it; it was probably begun in 1640 by Robert Hooke, a collaborator with Wren in his London work after the Great Fire.

PLATE 17 : EMMANUEL COLLEGE

We are in the Front Court and looking at the chapel designed by Sir Christopher Wren. The choice of architect was made by William Sandcroft. He had been Master of Emmanuel until he became Dean of St Paul's, where he was soon to be in close contact with Wren in the matter of rebuilding the cathedral. It was not unnatural for him to choose Wren to build the chapel of his college. A single chamber, some 60 feet long, runs the combined length of the façade and its attendant wings, surmounting the open cloister. This is known as the Long Gallery and its ostensible purpose was for the housing of portraits. The woodwork was done by Cornelius Austin, a Cambridge man. There is a ceiling, in good plaster-work of the period, by John Grove and an altar painting by Giacomo Amiconi, a Venetian artist who did a lot of work in England between 1729 and 1739. The subject is the Return of the Prodigal Son. The glass chandelier is also from Venice. It was intended in the first place that the façade of the Long Gallery was to have been of brick; stone from

Ketton is what we see today, admirably blending with the Westmoreland Building on the right. This was built in 1720 and, despite a fire which gutted it three years before our drawing was done, survives today in its original form. The arms of the noble family who subscribed £500 to the cost of this wing are to be seen over the central doorway – just 'out of picture' to the right. Had the artist included them in his drawing he would have had to leave out the Hall on the other side of the court. This is part of the original buildings put up soon after the foundation of the college in 1584 by Sir Walter Mildmay, Chancellor of the Exchequer to Queen Elizabeth. Although the great oriel window establishes its date, the character of the interior of the Hall today is due to the work of the Cambridge architect James Essex in 1760.[1] The college is not only an Elizabethan but a Puritan foundation. One of its most illustrious sons – and one who ran true to form – was John Harvard, founder of the university of that name in Cambridge, Massachusetts. Do not let us forget, also, Jeremy Taylor, author of *Holy Living* and *Holy Dying*, Fellow of the College and, one feels, its ideal product; and Lemuel Gulliver, Bachelor of Arts.

PLATE 18 : SIDNEY COLLEGE HALL

Sidney Sussex is the title of the College today. It was founded by the Lady Frances Sidney, dowager Countess of Sussex, and received its charter in 1596. The present appearance of the College is due to the remodelling it received in 1820, five years after the publication of our volumes. Its neo-Gothicized

1. Essex's best work in this college is in the façade to St. Andrew's Street, usually well set-off by the skilful planting of the flower-beds which front it, to the delight of travellers from the railway station who here encounter their first college.

Roman-cemented exterior has come in for some sharp criticism in its time but finds itself fashionable again today. Its transformer was Sir Jeffry Wyattville, who also took in hand the gothicizing of Windsor Castle. But there is nothing to be seen of this cult in our plate. In fact, the impeccable Italianate ceiling, put up about 1749 – when the wainscoting was also done – conceals, by all accounts, a late mediaeval hammer-beam roof. The best known member of the College was Oliver Cromwell. His death-mask, framed and curtained, hangs beside the High Table.

PLATE 19 : DOWNING COLLEGE

This is the latest foundation in the University – if we except Selwyn – and it was fourteen years old by charter and seven years advanced in building when Westall did this plate. The Master's Lodge and the Law Professor's Lodge were the only parts of the college which had been completed to Wilkins's designs. The immense area of the original site is seen very well; it extended as far as Pembroke, which we see in the distance, and the potentialities it offered for planning and planting on a park-like scale were realized from the beginning. The young trees, so carefully protected in our picture, have reached maturity and give distinction to what still remains of the College grounds today. But most of the land we see here is covered now by the complex of laboratories and scientific museums which mean 'Cambridge' to the modern world. The plan of the College, not fully realized today, is an ambitious one; the buildings, encased in Ketton stone, were to be ranged around a quadrangle almost as large as the Great Court of Trinity. In our plate – one of the best in the series – two salient features of the Cambridge sky-line, the immense floating mass of King's Chapel and the tower of the University

Church, show well under the typical midsummer East Anglian sky. One is made aware of the flatness of the encircling terrain and the proximity of the still half-reclaimed Fenlands is suggested by the alighting marsh-birds, of an unidentified species, upon the lush, well-watered sward.

PLATE 20: PUBLIC LIBRARY AND SENATE HOUSE

The Senate House is both the parliament house of the University and the place of honour where degrees are conferred. It was begun in 1722 to the designs of James Gibbs, architect of one of London's best-known churches, St Martin's-in-the-Fields, and of the two steeples in the Strand. The stone is Portland, the iron-balustrading on the east side – just out of view on the right – is of Sussex-smelted metal of a design and quality similar to that surrounding St Paul's Cathedral. The ornamented parts of the ceiling are by the Italians Artari and Bagutti and the execution of the woodwork was supervised by James Essex. Statues by Rysbrack of the Duke of Somerset, and by Nollekens of William Pitt, should not be overlooked. Here were enacted, at the time of our picture and for many years afterwards, the ceremonies attendant upon the examination for Tripos degree. A Tripos is an Honours degree, and takes its name from the three-legged stool upon which the examiner sat whilst disputing the thesis of an applicant. Until 1772 all examinations were orally conducted and attended by a critical and loquacious public. Written papers as we know them today were not introduced until the late eighteen-twenties. Degrees are conferred here, the postulant being presented to the Vice-Chancellor by the Father of his college – the Praelector – in the name of the Trinity. On great occasions, when honorary degrees are bestowed upon distinguished public men, it is the function of the Public Orator, always a classical scholar of repute, to compose and recite neat and laudatory addresses of welcome in Latin. Here, too, on major occasions, appear various other officers of the University. The Proctors, who are chiefly responsible for the maintenance of discipline, and their servants or constables, popularly known as 'Bull-dogs' (abbreviated to 'Bullers'), constitute the militant side of official surveillance over the morals of the student population. The Esquire Bedells, whose chief duty it is to accompany the Chancellor and Vice-Chancellor, may also be seen on ceremonial occasions.

The façade of the University Library (or Public Library as it is called in our plate to distinguish it from the ordinary college library) was added in 1754. For five hundred years or so this building performed the dual function of library and office for the University. The books accumulated and finally squeezed out the administrative side altogether. The Senate House was one of the results. But nothing could cope with the growth of the library until, in 1934, the huge collections were taken across the river to Sir Giles Gilbert Scott's new building, complete with skyscraper, and the old building reverted to offices. Cambridge University Library, together with the British Museum, the Bodleian Library at Oxford, the Scottish National Library at Edinburgh and Trinity College, Dublin, enjoys the privilege, under the Copyright Act, of receiving a copy of every new publication in the United Kingdom. This means an addition of about 14,000 books a year. The façade we see in our plate is exactly as it is today; it was finished in 1758 to the design of Stephen Wright. Beyond, peeping above the roof of the Senate House, is the cupola of the Gate of Honour in Caius College.

THE PLATES

1. St Peter's College (Peterhouse)

2. Clare Hall (Clare College)

3. *Pembroke Hall (Pembroke College)*

4. *Caius College*

5. Trinity Hall

6. King's College Chapel

7. *Catharine Hall Chapel (St Catharine's College)*

8. *Benet College Chapel (Corpus Christi College)*

9. *Queen's College (Queens' College)*

10. Christ College (Christ's College)

11. Trinity College Kitchen

12. *Trinity College Quadrangle (Great Court)*

13. Trinity College Library

14. *Jesus College*

15. *St John's College Second Court*

16. *Magdalen College Library (Magdalene College)*

17. *Emanuel College (Emmanuel College)*

18. *Sidney College Hall (Sidney Sussex College)*

19. Downing College

20. *Public Library (Old Schools) and Senate House*